HAL•LEONARD
INSTRUMENTAL PLAY-ALONG

ONLINE MEDIA INCLUDED
Audio Recordings
Printable Piano Accompaniments

PLAYBACK+
Speed • Pitch • Balance • Loop

CLASSICAL S... FOR TRUMPET

15 Easy Solos for Contest and Performance

Arranged by Philip Sparke

TITLE	PAGE
Waltz	2
Chorale (Now praise, my soul, the Lord)	3
Humming Song (from *Album for the Young*)	4
Gymnopédie No. 1	5
I'm Called Little Buttercup (from *HMS Pinafore*)	6
Study (Op. 37, No. 3)	7
Minuet (Z. 649)	8
Theme and Variation (from *Sonatina No. 3*)	9
Northern Song (from *Album for the Young*)	10
Two German Dances (from *12 German Dances, D. 420*)	11
Watchman's Song (from *Lyric Pieces, Op. 12*)	12
Gavotte	13
Vien quà, Dorina bella	14
Minuet (from *Notebook for Anna Magdalena Bach*)	15
The Prince of Denmark's March	16
B♭ Tuning Notes	

To access recordings and PDF accompaniments visit:
www.halleonard.com/mylibrary

Enter Code
7185-1331-2272-8519

ISBN 978-1-61780-700-8

Copyright © 2011 by HAL LEONARD CORPORATION
International Copyright Secured   All Rights Reserved

Visit Hal Leonard Online at
www.halleonard.com

Contact us:
Hal Leonard
7777 West Bluemound Road
Milwaukee, WI 53213
Email: info@halleonard.com

In Europe, contact:
Hal Leonard Europe Limited
42 Wigmore Street
Marylebone, London, W1U 2RN
Email: info@halleonardeurope.com

In Australia, contact:
Hal Leonard Australia Pty. Ltd.
4 Lentara Court
Cheltenham, Victoria, 3192 Australia
Email: info@halleonard.com.au

WALTZ

B♭ TRUMPET

MORITZ VOGEL
Arranged by PHILIP SPARKE

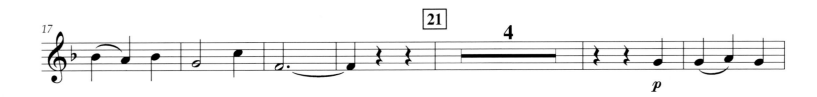

00842548

CHORALE

Now praise, my soul, the Lord

B♭ TRUMPET

JOHANN SEBASTIAN BACH
Arranged by PHILIP SPARKE

HUMMING SONG

from *Album for the Young*

Bb TRUMPET

ROBERT SCHUMANN
Arranged by PHILIP SPARKE

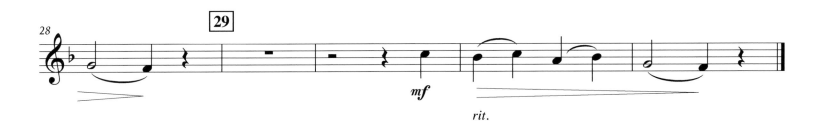

GYMNOPÉDIE NO. 1

Bb TRUMPET

ERIK SATIE
Arranged by PHILIP SPARKE

00842548

I'M CALLED LITTLE BUTTERCUP

from *HMS Pinafore*

Bb TRUMPET

SIR ARTHUR SULLIVAN
Arranged by PHILIP SPARKE

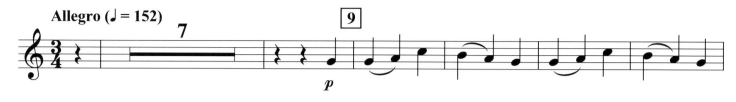

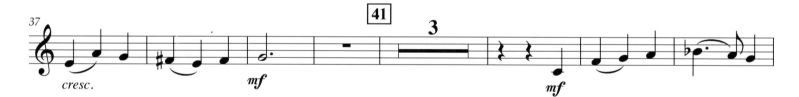

STUDY

Op. 37, No. 3

Bb TRUMPET

HENRY LEMOINE
Arranged by PHILIP SPARKE

00842548

MINUET
(Z. 649)

B♭ TRUMPET

HENRY PURCELL
Arranged by PHILIP SPARKE

THEME AND VARIATION

from *Sonatina No. 3*

B♭ TRUMPET

THOMAS ATTWOOD
Arranged by PHILIP SPARKE

Moderato (♩ = 104)

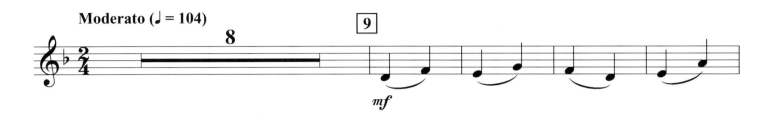

rit.

00842548

NORTHERN SONG

from *Album for the Young*

Bb TRUMPET

ROBERT SCHUMANN
Arranged by PHILIP SPARKE

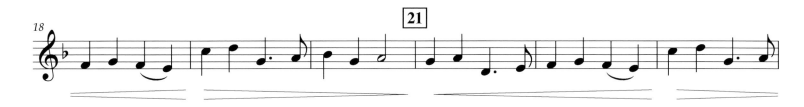

TWO GERMAN DANCES

from *Twelve German Dances, D. 420*

B♭ TRUMPET

FRANZ SCHUBERT
Arranged by PHILIP SPARKE

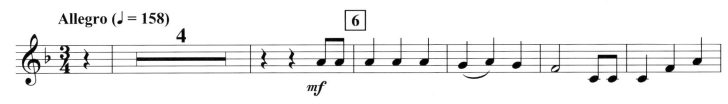

WATCHMAN'S SONG

from *Lyric Pieces, Op. 12*

B♭ TRUMPET

EDVARD GRIEG
Arranged by PHILIP SPARKE

Moderato (♩ = 104)

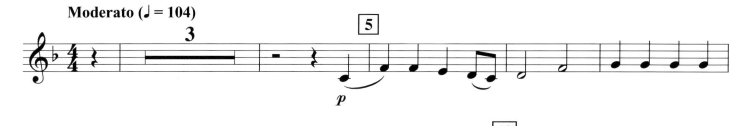

GAVOTTE

Bb TRUMPET

JAN LADISLAV DUSSEK
Arranged by PHILIP SPARKE

Allegro (♩ = 120)

VIEN QUÀ, DORINA BELLA

Bb TRUMPET

ANTONIO BIANCHI
Transcribed by **C. M. von WEBER**
Arranged by PHILIP SPARKE

Moderato (♩ = 96)

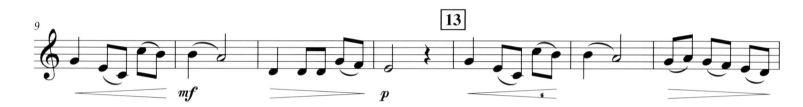

MINUET

from *Notebook for Anna Magdalena Bach*

B♭ TRUMPET

Attributed to **CHRISTIAN PETZOLD**
Arranged by PHILIP SPARKE

Moderato (♩ = 112)

00842548

THE PRINCE OF DENMARK'S MARCH

from *Choice Lessons for the Harpsichord or Spinet*

B♭ TRUMPET

JEREMIAH CLARKE
Arranged by PHILIP SPARKE

Moderato (♩ = 112)

(2nd time only)

rit.